The Little Mechaincs Alphabet Book

ABC's

Artwork designed by Authors

ISBN: 1448676193

Printed in the United States of America

My name is Boxy.

Do you know your Alphabet?

I want to help you learn about car parts too.

LET'S HAVE FUN!

The Little Mechanic's Alphabet Book ABC's

I am an automobile.

I use <u>brakes</u> to stop.

A **carburetor** mixes fuel with air so my engine will run.

My <u>driveshaft</u> delivers power to the rear end.

My <u>engine</u> is
where I get my power.

The <u>fuel</u> pump sends gasoline to the carburetor.

My <u>grille</u> makes me look different and lets air flow through.

My <u>headlights</u>
shine on the road.

My <u>ignition</u> sends power to the starter so my engine will start.

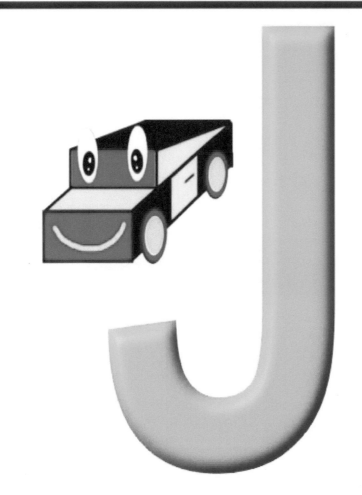

A <u>jack</u> is a device that is used to raise me off the ground.

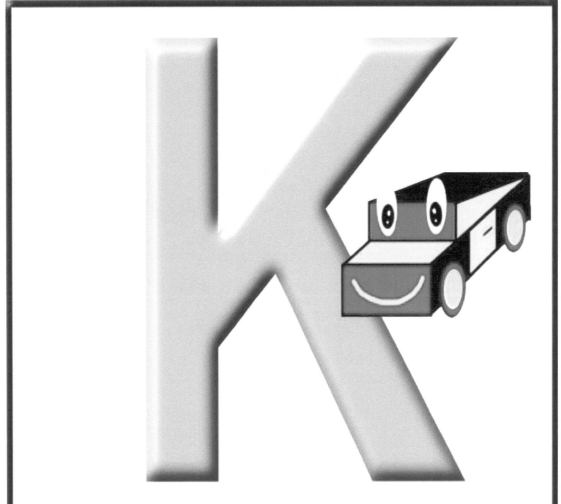

The **kingpin** is in the steering. It helps me turn my wheels.

A luggage rack is what I use to carry stuff.

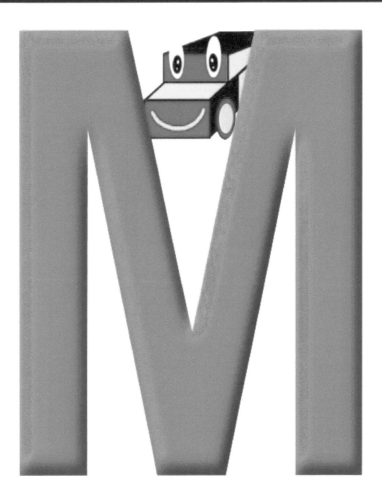

My <u>mirror</u> is used to see behind me.

A <u>nut</u> holds
my tire on.

The <u>odometer</u> keeps track of mileage.

The <u>piston</u> compresses gas and air inside the cylinder.

If I <u>quit</u> running
that means
something is wrong.

I have a <u>radio</u> so
I can listen to music.

The **starter** is what **starts** my engine.

I use my <u>tires</u> to
roll down the road.

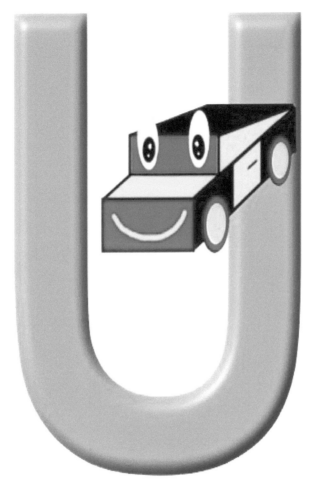

The <u>universal</u> joint allows rotary motion so my transmission will turn my axles.

Every vehicle has a VIN number. Wonder what mine is?

The **windshield** is so people can look outside at the road.

A <u>xXx</u> car chase
or an <u>X</u> for a kiss.

The <u>yoke</u> holds the universal joint.

Zoom means I can move fast.

CPSIA information can be obtained
at www.ICGtesting.com
Printed in the USA
LVHW070729200119
604507LV00029BA/729/P